# Leading the Way

Written by Kerrie Shanahan

**Flying Start**
to Literacy®

# Contents

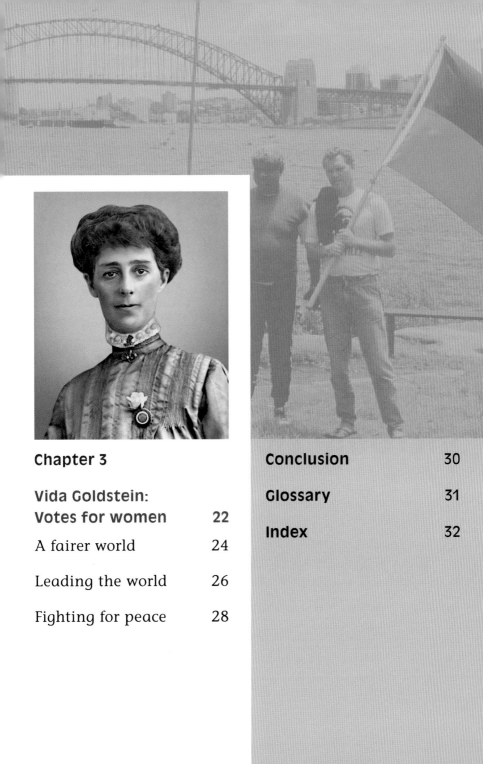

## Chapter 3

60c

East. Heath
Shore line
Looking

WABlood

2013

AUSTRALIA

Eddie "Koiki" Mabo 1936–92

# Introduction

Is there an issue you feel strongly about? Do you stand up for what you believe in? Are you passionate about making a difference?

When you are passionate about something, you often inspire others to join you and fight for a cause. Your passion encourages them to take action. This is how change happens. And this is what it means to be a leader. You may not have planned to be a leader, but you are!

These three people – Anh Do (left), Eddie Mabo (middle) and Vida Goldstein (right) have all made a difference.

Great leaders create change, and these changes make a difference in the world.

Here are the stories of three leaders who, with persistence, broke down barriers, inspired others and brought about change.

# Chapter 1
## Anh Do:
## A positive leader

Well-known actor, comedian, author and artist, Anh Do is lucky to be alive!  When Anh was only two years old, his family made an incredible escape from Vietnam and came to Australia as **refugees**.  Growing up in a new country was difficult, but Anh Do has become an inspiring role model and a leader in the community.

Ho Chi Minh City, southern Vietnam, in the 1970s

## Escape

Anh was born in Vietnam in 1977. His family were very poor and they lived in a small house with fourteen other family members.

A few years before Anh was born, the long war between North and South Vietnam had come to an end. During the war, Australia sent soldiers to help the South Vietnamese fight against the North. Anh's uncles fought alongside Australian soldiers.

In 1975, North Vietnam won the war and united the country. The new government punished many southern Vietnamese people, including their families, who fought against them. Anh's family had no choice, but to flee their country. If they didn't, they could have been killed.

# A new start

Anh and his family crammed onto a small wooden boat with over forty people, and escaped out to sea.

For five days, Anh and his family encountered many threats.  Wild storms battered their small boat.  They were twice held up by pirates who stole all of their possessions – even the boat's motor.  And they ran out of food and fresh water.

Just as it appeared that the refugees were doomed, a German ship found them and took them to safety.

A group of Vietnamese refugees wait to be rescued from a fishing boat

**Did you know?**
Before 1976, there were
very few Vietnamese
people in Australia.
By 1981, there were
over 2,000 Vietnamese
refugees living here.

Anh and his family eventually ended up in Sydney, Australia. This was the beginning of their new life, but their new life was hard. They had to understand a new language, and different **customs** and **traditions**. Also, Anh's family were very poor, so his parents had to work extremely hard to provide for them.

At school, Anh faced challenges, too. He spoke Vietnamese, and learning to read and write in English was hard.

He also had trouble making friends. Some of the other kids teased Anh because he looked different from them, and they laughed at his food and his clothes. They didn't know Anh's family couldn't afford a school uniform for him to wear.

# A positive outlook

Even though Anh faced difficult times, he was thankful to be safe in Australia:

*"I could have been an orphan. So many things could have gone wrong but here I am … I realise how lucky I am to be here."*

Anh's parents taught him to be grateful, no matter how tough things got. They wanted Anh to do well at school and to "give back" to the country that took his family in when they had nowhere else to go.

> "You listen to us, kids. As you grow up, make sure you do as much as you can to give back to this country that gave us a second chance."
>
> Anh Do's parents, *The Happiest Refugee*

Anh wanted his parents to be proud of him. He worked hard and became a good student.

When Anh was thirteen, his father left the family home. This was a difficult time, and Anh's family were now even poorer. Anh helped his mother by doing extra work at home.

St Aloysius College, Kirribilli, Sydney,
where Anh Do went to secondary school

Anh worked hard at secondary school and even though he couldn't afford text books, he did very well. After finishing school, Anh went to university to study law. The young boy who had struggled to read and write, was going to become a lawyer!

But in his final year at university, Anh decided to take a different path.

# Inspiring others

Anh began doing comedy routines at local comedy clubs. The audience liked him – they laughed! He realised he was good at it, so he decided performing would be his career, not law. It was a risk, but Anh was brave:

*"... you lose and fail, but you still celebrate ... because you've given it a red-hot go. There is no need to fear failure."*

Anh performed more and more comedy and acting jobs, and at times he faced **racism**. Some people didn't like that he was "different" and successful. But this didn't deter Anh. His popularity grew and he appeared on many TV programs – becoming one of the first Vietnamese-born people to do so.

Anh has written many books too, including his biography, *The Happiest Refugee*. Anh's books help people to understand life as a refugee living in a new country.

Anh uses comedy, honesty and great story-telling to share the issues faced by refugees. This breaks down barriers between people and changes the views some people have about people from different cultures.

Like his parents had hoped, Anh "gives back". He donates time and money to various charities, including a charity in Vietnam that provides for children who do not have shelter, food and education.

From almost dying at sea, Anh Do has become an inspiring leader!

Vietnamese children catching fish to sell. In Vietnam, some children don't go to school because they have to work to support their families.

# Chapter 2
# Eddie Koiki Mabo:
# Fighting for change

Indigenous Australian peoples have been living in Australia for tens of thousands of years. About 240 years ago, people from Europe sailed to Australia. When they arrived, they claimed the land as their own, even though hundreds of thousands of Indigenous peoples were living in Australia. This was because of a concept known as *terra nullius*, which means "land that belongs to no one". How do you think this made Indigenous peoples feel?

When Eddie Koiki Mabo found out that his home did not belong to him, he was shocked.

> *"My family has occupied this land for hundreds of years before Captain Cook was born. They are now trying to say I cannot own it."*

**Did you know?**
*Terra nullius* is Latin for "nobody's land". In law, it means an uninhabited territory belonging to no state.

## Early activism

Eddie was born on Mer (Murray Island), an island in the Torres Strait, off the top end of Queensland. During Eddie's childhood, he learnt all about the land and the sea, and the beliefs of his people. He grew up immersed in the ways of his people and their **culture**.

When Eddie was twenty, he went to the mainland and worked in Queensland. He had several jobs, including building railways, cutting sugarcane and working on pearling boats. During these years, Eddie joined the Workers Union to fight for equal pay and fair conditions for Indigenous peoples. He encouraged other Indigenous workers to join the union, too.

15

Tree and landscape,
painted by
Eddie Mabo.
In his spare time,
Eddie enjoyed painting.

## Family and community

Eddie married Bonita Neehow, known as Netta, in 1959. Together they set up the Black Community School in Townsville so that Indigenous children could be taught about their culture, language and history – things that weren't taught at the local state school.

These were busy times for Eddie and Netta, and their family of ten children.

# Discrimination

Throughout Eddie's life, he was treated differently to white people. He faced discrimination because of the colour of his skin. For example, he wasn't allowed to enter the cinema through the same door as white people. And sometimes he heard people telling jokes and laughing about him, just because he was black.

All of these things increased Eddie's desire to create change – to make things fair for his people. Eddie became a leader in several organisations: he was Chairman of the Indigenous Housing Co-operative and Secretary for the Queensland Aborigines Advancement League.

As a young man, Eddie worked on pearling boats. This was one of the many jobs he did where Indigenous workers were paid less than white workers.

# Defining moments

In 1973, Eddie began working as a gardener at James Cook University in Townsville. He loved reading in the library during his breaks and sitting in on classes, and it was here that he met and became friends with Noel Loos and Henry Reynolds, who taught at the university.

One day, when the three friends were chatting, Noel and Henry realised that Eddie assumed he owned his land on Mer and would one day return to it. They explained to Eddie that by law it wasn't his land – it legally belonged to the government, and at any time it could be taken away from him and the people living there. Eddie was stunned. "No way! It's not theirs, it's ours," he argued. And he vowed to fight this injustice!

In Memory Of
**EDWARD KOIKI MABO**

BORN MURRAY ISLAND 29 - 6 - 1936
DIED 21 - 1 - 1992
AGED 56 YEARS

LOVING HUSBAND OF BONITA
DEVOTED FATHER, FATHER-IN-LAW
GRANDFATHER, BROTHER,
BROTHER-IN-LAW, UNCLE AND FRIEND

HE WAS A KNOWN AND RESPECTED MEMBER IN LOCAL,
STATE AND NATIONAL ORGANISATIONS.
HIS INVOLVEMENT IN BLACK AFFAIRS DATES BACK TO
THE EARLY 1960'S. THE MOST IMPORTANT ONE WAS THE
MURRAY ISLAND LAND CLAIM KNOWN AS "MABO CASE".
HE PUT SO MUCH OF HIS STRENGTH, HIS INSPIRATION,
HIS FIGHTING SPIRIT AND HIS WISDOM INTO THE CASE,
WHICH HAS PROFOUND SIGNIFICANCE, NOT ONLY FOR
THE MURRAY ISLANDERS, BUT ALSO FOR THE TORRES
STRAIT ABORIGINAL PEOPLE AND INDIGENOUS PEOPLE
EVERYWHERE.

" A MERIAM MAN OF PIADARAM CLAN "
ALWAYS LOVED.

**Did you know?**
The library at James Cook University in Townsville was renamed the Eddie Mabo Library.

Eddie's family has lived on Mer, an island in the Torres Strait, for many generations.

A few years later, Eddie was giving a talk about **land rights** at the university.  He explained how the Indigenous people of Mer had been passing down the land they lived on through their families from generation to generation since the beginning of time.  A lawyer listening in the audience suggested that Eddie should make a land rights claim in the courts.

This was the beginning of a ten-year legal battle – a battle to which Eddie would dedicate the rest of his life.

# A long battle

In 1982, Eddie and a group of Indigenous people from Mer, began their legal fight to overturn *terra nullius*, and be awarded legal ownership of their land. It was a tough legal battle. Some of Eddie's fellow islanders left the group because they were worried that if the case failed, they could lose their homes forever. Eddie and his family received threats from people who opposed what they were doing. But Eddie persevered.

And then, Eddie received the terrible news that he had cancer. Sadly, he died in January 1992. He died without knowing if he had won the court case.

The court announced their historic decision five months after Eddie's death, on 3 June 1992. It ruled that the lands of the Australian continent were not *terra nullius,* or "land belonging to no one", when Europeans colonised Australia. The court voted that the land belonged to its traditional owners. Eddie had won – not just for himself, but for his people!

**Did you know?**
Each year on 3 June, Mabo Day is celebrated to remember Eddie and the landmark court decision.

A year later, the government passed a law called the *Native Title Act 1993*, which made it easier for Indigenous peoples to claim land rights. The court decision that Eddie had fought so hard to win, has become known as "Mabo". Eddie Mabo changed history, and left a lasting legacy for all of us.

## Native Title Act 1993

The main objects of this Act are:

(a) to provide for the recognition and protection of native title; and

(b) to establish ways in which future dealings affecting native title may proceed and to set standards for those dealings; and

(c) to establish a mechanism for determining claims to native title; and

(d) to provide for, or permit, the validation of past acts, and intermediate period acts, invalidated because of the existence of native title.

Part 1—Preliminary, 3 Objects

# Chapter 3
# Vida Goldstein:
# Votes for women

When you look at the world around you, it is normal to think: "Things have always been this way, and they will always be this way." But that is not true. The way things are – such as rules and laws – were created by people, and they can be changed.

In the late 1800s, there was a law that only men could vote in elections. It was one of those things that seemed to have always been that way and would never change.

But a woman named Vida Goldstein thought differently. Her mother, Isabella, strongly believed that women should vote, and Vida agreed. In 1891, when Vida was just 22, she joined with her mother and other women to collect signatures for a **petition** they would present to the government of Victoria. Although they collected 30,000 signatures in support of women's right to vote, this petition did not succeed. But Vida was inspired to keep fighting for the right of women to vote.

23

# A fairer world

For Vida, this was the start of a lifelong effort to make the world a fairer place. Before she turned 30, Vida became leader of a group called the United Council for Woman Suffrage. ("Suffrage" means "the right to vote".) This group was at the forefront of fighting to extend the vote to women.

In 1902, women in Australia were granted the right to vote and to stand for **Commonwealth Parliament**. So, in 1903, Vida decided to run for office. She was one of the first women in the world to stand for election. It would be the first of five attempts, all of which failed. But in each election, she was able to speak up about important issues, such as seeking peace between nations and promoting social fairness.

Vida also travelled around the world to encourage women's rights in other countries. In 1902, she travelled throughout Europe and to the United States to help organise people in their fight for women's voting rights.

**Did you know?**
In 1893, New Zealand was the first country in the world to grant the vote to all women. In 1902, Australia was the first country to grant women both the right to vote and the right to stand for parliament.

NEW ZEALAND

WOMEN'S SUFFRAGE 1893

40c

Flyer advertising the Women's Coronation Procession on Saturday 17 June, 1911, in England. Vida Goldstein was one of the speakers.

# Leading the world

Australia and New Zealand were the first countries in the world to allow women to vote. This was because Vida and many others decided to challenge the way things had always been done. Vida worked tirelessly to make Australia a leader in women's voting rights.

It would be another decade before women could vote in the United States and 20 years before women had full voting rights in the United Kingdom.

A cartoon from the United Kingdom Suffrage League, 1909.
Jane:    "Give me a bit of the voting cookie, Johnnie."
Johnnie: "It wouldn't be good for you."
Jane:    "How can you tell if you won't let me try it? It doesn't hurt those other little girls."

Women march for the right to vote in New York City, USA, in 1916.

However, the fight for women's rights wasn't won by all women – only white women were allowed to vote. Indigenous Australians were denied the right to vote until 1962.

The work to make the world a fairer place is never finished. There are always injustices that need to be fixed. Even today, there are some countries that still deny or restrict the right to vote for women or various racial or ethnic groups.

After white women won the right to vote in Australia, Vida continued to work to address other issues such as international conflict.

# Fighting for peace

In 1914, the world descended into World War I.  The war involved more than 100 countries and 70 million military personnel.  More than 22 million people – including 13 million **civilians** – died during the war.

Vida was against violence of any kind – she was a pacifist. She argued against **drafting** Australians into the war and worked to ensure that women and children were properly cared for while men were overseas fighting.  She also argued that men and women should be paid the same amount for the same work.

A women's peace parade, shortly after the start of World War I

**Did you know?**
Women workers were granted equal pay in Australia in 1969 and New Zealand in 1972. This aims to ensure all workers are paid equally, based on the value of their work and skill without any regard to their gender. However, today, many women still earn less than men.

The lesson of Vida Goldstein is clear. When you look around and see the world as it is, don't assume it has to be that way. Where you see injustice, you can work to make change. It might not be easy, or quick, but you can have a role in making the world a better place.

# Conclusion

Some leaders are passionate about their beliefs and they share this passion with others. They fight for what they believe in and persevere to create change.

Some people become leaders because they are the first to do something. This breaks down barriers, and makes it easier for others to follow in their footsteps.

Many leaders are inspirational. They motivate others to work with them, and they make a positive difference to their community.

Leaders have different qualities, but they all have one thing in common – the ability to draw people in, hold their attention and inspire them to act.

# Glossary

**civilians** people who are not a member of the police, military or firefighting force

**Commonwealth Parliament** the Federal Government in Australia that makes laws for all of Australia

**culture** a way of life shared by people in a place or time

**customs** long-established practices shared by a group of people

**drafting** to select people for compulsory military service

**land rights** the right to possess land; especially the rights of the original inhabitants of a country to possess their traditional land

**petition** a written request signed by many people who support a shared cause or concern

**racism** believing that one race of people is better than another race; treating people unfairly because of their race

**refugees** people who have to leave their county because their life is in danger if they stay there

**traditions** ways of doing things that a group of people pass on to their children, who then pass them on to their children, and so on

# Index